AM I ALLOWED TO BE A KID

AM I ALLOWED TO BE A KID

The Experiences of an American Teenager

LAUREN TO

FUTURE
MEDIA, LLC

To Future Media LLC

CONTENTS

This book is dedicated to my very wonderful family who has supported and loved me every step of the way: my mother, Regina To, and my father, Youngchan To, as well as my two younger siblings, Andrew To and Kristen To.

I would also like to dedicate this book to all of the special people who have also supported me: my Godmother, Lori Levya, along with some of my favorite people, Cynda Tyler and Deb Schmidt. And I could never forget about my co-editor Billy McClellan. Finally, I'd also like to dedicate this book to my school, Arrowhead Park Early College High School, and the amazing teachers and principal there.

Introduction

Hi! My name is Lauren To, and I am a 14-year-old girl living in a small city in the U.S. If you want to learn why teenagers sometimes act the way we do, keep reading. If you don't, well you've already started, haven't you? Fair warning, I'm writing about how it feels being a kid in today's society based on my *personal* experiences.

To some people, 14 sounds like a big number, but when I'm comparing it to all of the amazing, and not-so-great people I've seen and heard about, I'd say it's a pretty reasonable number to still consider "child-age". I am also a sophomore attending Arrowhead Park Early College High School, a public school. For those who don't know or can't remember the terminology, I'm a tenth grader. Pretty young, huh? When I was in elementary school, I took third and fourth grade in the same year, though that's a bit confusing to explain, so I usually just say I skipped fourth grade. To be honest, I sort of feel like I'm growing up a little faster than expected. Some might say that it's because I skipped a grade, but I don't really feel like that's the case. I think the issue is society.

Now give me a minute before you come at me with your torches and pitchforks. When I say society, I don't mean the overused stereotype about how high school is so difficult and it's hard to fit in, but my actual experiences outside of school. In other words, I think the issues are all of the experiences I have -- and don't have.

In addition to that, it sometimes feels like life is on repeat. Every time I turn my head, the conversation is either about politics, Tik-

Tok, or that one random school fight that happened months ago. Not only that, but sometimes it feels like I'm constantly being told to grow up fast. Why would I want to grow up fast? I'm living a pretty good life right now. All I have to do is exist to survive. I'm going to say this once, so listen up the people in the back, I am a freeloader. And if I'm being truthful, I don't mind.

But it feels like people are constantly telling me, grow up, make money, be successful, work hard, etc. To be honest it sometimes feels like a bit too much. I feel like my biggest question should be, what do I want to do after I finish my school work? Not, am I doing enough to live a happy life?

Though when I think about it, all of my thoughts are influenced by who and why I am who I am. Why do I think this way? Why don't we think the same? Who is Lauren To? Great questions, with long answers. Thankfully though, we have a whole book to answer those questions. So, without further ado, let's get this show on the road.

Chapter 1 | Pack Life

Here's the story of my life. First, I was born. After that, I was subjected to society's stereotypes. The end.

Not really, I'm joking. Kind of.

To begin (for real this time), let's start with 'normal'. What is normal?

Here's my answer, 'normal doesn't exist'.

You may be thinking, that's a load of bull, being normal is this and that, and honestly, I couldn't care less. Calling people normal is a way for insecure people to cement their status or role in a group and to alienate other people who they believe stand out in a way that's different from them. People naturally want to belong to a group and that's fine, however what I find ridiculous is that the English language has over 150,000 words, and we choose to ignore all that and generalize people under one word.

The common thought is that being normal means that you're average. Anything below that is not normal and anything above that is also not normal. Opinions aside, everyone wants to belong, usually to a group. Normal is just one standard that people (especially kids) use to separate themselves from people who are different. Calling other kids names like 'freak' or 'loser' implies that they're not the same as their peers and are different in a bad way. Just the negative connotation of those words is enough to illustrate the impact that being "not-normal" can have. When that happens, kids who may have been excited about whatever they're doing can be discouraged, and that follows them for a long time. Not only that, but those kids who are "not-normal" will push down their talents just for a chance to fit in. It's a soul-crushing mindset, and it's not one that is easily breakable.

Even as a teenager, just the thought of being ostracized is enough to make me stop and seriously hesitate over whether I want to be my own person and stand out in the crowd. Everyone tries so hard to not stand out, and for what? So they don't have to worry about standing by themself, or sitting by themself at lunch? Concept wise, the idea is a bit ridiculous, but in reality, it's terrifying and very real.

Want to know the easiest way to make a kid lose their confidence and suppress their interests? Tell them that they're not normal. That is how much power the word 'normal' has, and honestly, I'm not okay with that.

In addition to using normalcy as an excuse to alienate other kids, normalcy can also affect people's perception of themselves, which doesn't make sense to me because every person is different. Some kids may be horrible in school but have amazing artistic talent. Others may do great in school, but have a hard time making friends. It is impossible to generalize everybody under one word. I have friends who can light up a room with their smile but cannot sit down and finish a book for the life of them. I also have friends who could outsmart anyone even on a bad day, but have a hard time making new friends. I could never imagine calling them normal, because they're not. They're all amazing and unique. Not only that, but if everyone was the exact same, I'd lose my mind with boredom.

But sometimes, I just want to blend into the crowd because it's comfortable. Not standing out is the perfect way for me to not draw attention to myself. So, I act like the majority, in terms of speech and personality – or I try too at least. And I just recently learned that it is important to be yourself. However, it can be hard, because you have to stand out in the crowd and draw attention to yourself. Sadly, some people don't like that and things like bullying can occur because of that. That's why so many people are scared to be themselves, they want to be 'normal' and they don't want to be different. But there's one fatal flaw to this very popular mindset: every person is different.

People each have their own unique personality with traits that could never be found exactly in anyone else. Even the idea of trying to take that away from people just so that they could fit it doesn't seem to make much sense. Not only is every person their own self, but also because the world moves and evolves because people are different. Due to people's differences as a society, we've learned and studied only to become better and better.

On that note, it also never made sense to me to pick on people when they don't fit the stereotype of being 'normal'. That is unreasonable, especially when some turn to shaming teenagers.

Everybody is different. Just because a teenager isn't the exact same as a different teenager (maybe even younger you) doesn't mean that there is something wrong with them. Times change, and people need to change too. If I'm putting my honest opinion out there, I think that most people would be even more upset with their kid if they acted just like their parents.

So many people spend so much time chasing after this image of normalcy because it's safe and comfortable blending into the crowd, but normalcy is an illusion. Most kids try to be normal because they just don't want to stand out and want to live their lives in peaceful misery. However, picking on kids who don't want to follow that path is not only unreasonable, but also cowardly. Unless that kid/teenager is placing themself or others in danger, they have the right to become their own person and define who they are.

Here's another idea that also comes to mind when the word 'normal' is brought up; expectations and standards. There's this standard that we all set, unconsciously for the most part, that we judge people by. For the people that do better than that, we associate words to them that can negatively affect them; words like 'smart', 'try-hard', and 'naturally intelligent'. It's the same for the kids who don't meet our expectations. I'm not sure how many times I have to say this but everyone is different. It's illogical to judge everyone by the same standard, especially when not everyone has the same starting point.

Some kids have better access to resources, while others may struggle to even attend school period. Some may be better at studying, while others may have an abundance of "street smarts". Every person has their own special set of talents, meaning that it makes no sense to try to hold everyone to the same standard. Of course, there should be a baseline standard for behavior and basic human skills, but in terms of the finer details there should be more flexibility.

Sure, that kid may not be so good at math, but they can draw pictures with an imagination overflowing with creativity, an imagination the math kid may never have. That means that everyone has their skills, and no one deserves to be outcasted or treated differently from their peers because of that.

And with that. I'd like to elaborate on my 'smart' comment. The reality is even separating kids from their peers in 'positive' ways can have negative results. As I've said over and over again, kids just want to belong, and regardless of whether you think that you're separating a kid from their group for positive or negative reasons, that person is still being separated. The sad truth is people are always going to be separated by their faults, however, anything that we can do to make the world a little better of a place for people should be done. One thing that we can try to do is not judge people who we perceive to be 'not-normal'.

I am not normal. I was the 'over-achiever', 'smart kid', and [my personal favorite] 'the weird kid'. I am proud of those names. I earned them. Being "not-normal" is just a mean way of saying unique. In fact, some of the most memorable people I have ever met were not considered normal. But what was fine for me is not the same for other kids. That's why so many kids act irrationally. It's not an action to disappoint the people around them, but a defense mechanism. That's why we feel safe in groups, and why some have 'generic' personalities.

When we sit down and think about it, the entire idea of normalcy stemmed from humanity's need to be part of a group. It's natural to want to belong. However, ostracizing others who we deem as 'not-normal' is not fine in the slightest. Everyone is different, and because of those differences humanity has managed to accomplish astounding things. Though having that sense of belonging may be comforting, the fact of the matter is that the only people who are remembered are the ones who are different. They're the ones who chose not to follow society's norms and conform to the idea of being 'normal'.

To restate my entire chapter, being normal is overrated. Though normal is comforting because of the literal group attached, everyone is different, and that's amazing. Without everyone's differences, there would be no advancements in society. There would be no change, no excitement.

Chapter 2 | Do You Eat Dogs ft. Racism

Before you ask, no, I do not eat dogs. I have never eaten a dog, or a cat, or even an alligator [which I hear tastes like chicken]. Usually, I just go right into the chapter, but this chapter is special. This one is about stereotypes and racism, specifically toward Asian-Americans.

I am an Asian-American. I was born and raised in the United States of America. And let me tell you, I've heard some dumb stuff in my life, but what's in this chapter, really takes the cake.

As an Asian-American I get a lot of questions that my white counterparts would never get. Such as, 'Where are you from?' or to be more specific, 'Are you Chinese?'. A personal favorite of mine, 'Do you eat dogs?'. But, going back to the first question, I've been asked this question so many times, that this had me thinking. What countries do people know are in Asia? So, I went and I asked my friend, 'What countries do you think are in Asia?'.

Their response, 'China, Japan, and Korea'.

They said it with so much confidence too. Of course, I had to make sure though, so I said, 'That's all?'.

Then, they nodded and told me, 'Yup!'.

At this point I'm dying [figuratively], so I knew I just had to go a little further, so I asked them, 'So, what do you think of when you think of Asia?'.

And they said, I [pardon my French] shit you not, 'Chinese food, anime, and Kpop'. It was at that moment where I realized...they did not know where India is. Oh, and they had no idea that there are over 45 countries in Asia.

Though, let's not come at my friend though. It was a genuinely hilarious experience, and I know that their answers were not a result of any sort of malice toward me or the Asian community.

Another thing that I find hilarious is the fact that random people, usually white middle-aged women*, think that it's okay to casually come up to me in public and ask me things like, 'Where are you from?' only to follow up with a 'Your English is so good!', or even better, when I tell them that I'm from America, 'No, where are you REALLY from?'. Calm down Karen, I already told you.

Usually though, I love giving snarky remarks. Saying things like, 'Where are YOU from?', or 'Your English is so good!', or a favorite of mine 'My mother's loins'. Which, while I find very entertaining, am still unsure as to the validity of that statement.

*This is not an attack against white people, nor middle-aged women, this is just a descriptive for an experience that I had that I am recalling. It could've been any random person of different age, ethnicity, or gender, but this is what I experienced.

Now, for the people who think that that is rude, I should respect my elders and all that jazz, you are the problem.

Think of the situation from my point of view. I am a child, that has just been randomly approached by a person I have never met nor heard of before and they come up to me and ask me a question which is 1.) none of their business and 2.) none of their concern. To be frank, I find these kinds of people annoying. And on the days where I decide to answer the questions minus the snark, my answer is almost always followed by this question, 'No, I meant where are your parents from?'. How is that any of their concern? Mind your own business and walk away. Apparently, it's perfectly acceptable to walk up to a random Asian and ask them that question, but it's not fine if I walk up to a random white person and ask them their heritage. That's whack.

Thankfully, I was raised surrounded by very educated people so I didn't have to deal with this often, but occasionally I would have the chance to interact with people who did not seem to be very educated. I try to let people know when they're being racist, but usually, I get shut down. It can be a little upsetting when I try to raise awareness for this kind of subtle racism only to be shut down with a couple comments pertaining to overreacting.

Not only that but as a teenager, comments like 'where are you really from' make me feel like I somehow don't belong in this country. I know that most people ask this question with some form of innocence, but even still, it's harmful, especially for younger Asians.

Another stereotype about Asians that just seems to completely baffle me is the idea that all Asians know each other. There's this sort of assumption from some people I've met that all Asians know each other. And I would imagine it's a little worse where I live just because there aren't a lot of Asians near where I live.

Don't believe me? Let's take a walk down memory lane.

One day I was at the mall with my friends. They both stepped away to do their own things and I was looking around the shop. All of a sudden, this white, middle-aged woman* came up to me and stared at me. At that point, I was just confused, and a little scared, because stranger danger. Due to the fact that I have no survival instincts, I turned toward her and said, "Yes?".

*Once again, this is not an attack against white people, nor middle-aged women, this is just a descriptive for an experience that I had that I am recalling. It could've been any random person of different age, ethnicity, or gender, but this is what I experienced.

She then had the audacity to ask me, "Do you know *insert name here*?".

Please keep in mind I have never seen this lady before in my life.

Of course, I go, "No.", then continue looking around.

She then tells me, "Oh, it's just because they're also Asian and I thought you might know each other. See, because I'm their mom's friend, something something" [she didn't really say 'Something something', I just stopped paying attention].

I then walked away. But that entire experience was weird. First of all, this random lady approached me, a child, because she thought I knew another person. Now that I think about it, she was probably a pedophile and/or slightly racist. But anyway, the entire situation was confusing and a little alarming. I would like to end this conversation here but I've also, unfortunately, had people I know ask me if I knew other Asians they knew.

It was the first day of Freshman year and I was introducing myself to some new people. I was talking to this girl, let's call her Bridgette. All of a sudden, Bridgette says to me, "Can I ask you a question?".

I reply, "Yeah, of course."

Bridgette says, "Do you know *insert name here*?"

"No, why do you ask?"

She then says, "Oh it's because she's also Asian so I thought you two may know each other?"

My response? "Why? Where do they even live?"

"Michigan."

How am I supposed to know a random Asian person in Michigan? I've never even been to Michigan before. I'm half convinced she believed Asians just have a hotline to every Asian on the planet.

It was definitely an experience, let me tell you that. However, I know that this girl was not purposefully trying to be racist. What she was doing was being microaggressive, meaning that she wasn't trying to be racist, but because of whatever factors, she grew up thinking that those kinds of questions were legitimate and appropriate. I see this a lot and it's, unfortunately, a lot more common than you think.

One area where I specifically see a lot of microaggressions and structural racism is in regards to academics. I'm sure everyone knows that Asians are stereotypically super smart and good at school. And while some kids may love to experience that, I hated it. When I was young, it always felt as if I had this extra weight on my shoulders because the teachers were just expecting that extra mile from me.

It does not feel great to have everyone expect the best or worst from you just because of your race. Yes, I'm Asian. But that doesn't mean I'm automatically amazing at math. I can do badly on tests too. I sometimes need reassurance from the adults around me. Believe it or not, it's hard for a 7-year-old to have confidence in themselves when whenever they accomplish something, they're constantly told by the people around them, 'To be expected', or even worse, 'You can do better'.

It's hard for a child to gain confidence and work harder when all of their efforts are undermined. The worst feeling is when a kid does something – the exact same thing that their friend has done—and their friend is the only one given praises. It sounds absurd, but it happens all the time. I can tell you tens of stories from both experience and observations of instances where an Asian kid and their friend (of a different race) have done the same thing and the amount of support is glaringly unequally distributed.

One example that comes to mind is when I was in 2nd grade.

In second grade, I had written a book (a short little children's book), and I worked with my friend (who was not Asian), we'll call her Lisa. I wrote the book and Lisa drew the pictures. We worked on the book for a couple of weeks and then when we finally finished, we showed it to our teacher, teachers if we count the teaching assistant.

When we showed them the book, their reactions were sort of heartbreaking. They praised Lisa for her drawing skills [which were amazing] and then essentially just showered her in compliments. On the other hand, they gave me a pat on the back and said 'Cool'. It hurt a little, not going to lie.

It may sound like I'm just complaining and whining about not being complimented, and to be honest, at first that may have been it. But that behavior continued over the course of that school year. When Lisa and I would accomplish equal things, the amount of support that was distributed by the teachers was not equal.

Now, don't get me wrong, I loved my second grade teachers. They are amazing people and great teachers. The thing is, sometimes the way we act towards others isn't based on hate but rather on instinct-which is based on what society and that person's experiences deem as acceptable.

Another example that I can remember, is actually not my personal experience, but rather one of my observations.

I remember watching these two kids at a daycare, and I say this in the least creepy way possible. I was there to pick up my little sister. Anyways, they looked like they were in third grade and they were both girls. One girl was Asian and the other was white. I was close enough to overhear their conversation and that's when I realized they were working on math homework. They had both raised their hands to ask for help and the daycare worker came over and helped the white girl and when the Asian girl piped in to ask a question the daycare worker looked genuinely surprised. I remember the worker saying something along the lines of, "Oh, I didn't expect that. I thought you already knew, I'm sorry about that".

These kinds of incidents occur a lot and they're usually in very minor situations. Most people don't actually notice that what they're saying is racist and it's not their fault. I notice that most people have no idea how racist some of their actions are until I point it out, and it's really sad that I have to point it out. Not only that, but it breaks my heart when I see situations like the last one happen to kids because they don't deserve that. Having the weight of the world on your shoulders and having people make assumptions about you just because of your race is a feeling that nobody deserves, especially children.

In fact, I loathe the entire idea of under- or over-estimating kids based on their race. I have met some of the most brilliant Black and Hispanic people in my life and whenever they accomplish anything remotely good, the people around them act as if it's a miracle, or even worse, dumb luck. That makes me so angry. Why are they underestimating these kids? They're amazing, and it can be hard watching how they're being treated.

On a bit of a happier note, I would also like to note that not all Asians are great at school. Now you could take my word for it (or literally any other Asian's on this planet) or take my dad's. Here's the conversation my dad overheard between two Korean girls at an airport.

One of them said to the other, in Korean, "Isn't the capital of the US, New York?".

The other girl responded with, "No, you idiot. It's LA".

I don't know about you, but if that was considered smart, I'm the next Einstein.

Also, most Asians aren't just born smart. We work hard, and our results happen to show it. On a side note, the capital of the US is Washington D.C. Not to be confused with Washington, especially since they are located on opposite sides of the US.

Though back to all seriousness, I would have to say, my least favorite part of being Asian is the FACT that racism overall towards Asians is not seen as a major problem and is sometimes even seen as socially acceptable.

Should it be socially acceptable to call someone 'ching-chong' (an Asian slur) or make fun of their eyes? It shouldn't, but it is. It isn't funny to be called 'ching-chong' or to have someone make fun of your eyes, but it happens so often, it's not seen as a major problem. As a matter of fact, I have even gotten bullied for my features.

When I was in elementary school, I was bullied by this one guy, we'll call him Tim.

Tim was an idiot. He thought it was funny to make fun of my eyes, which are slanted and small. He would say crap about how my eyes were small and essentially just make fun of them. It was not fun. The saddest thing about it though was the fact that when I told the teachers they brushed it off, and the issue was tabled until my dad had to come to the school and talk to the principal about it.

Many Asians don't have parents who are able to do what my dad did. Some have accents that they're embarrassed of, don't have the time, or just cannot step in for whatever reason. So, that kind of bullying just continues until the bully gets bored or grows up.

I've already discussed a couple of specific examples regarding Asian racism, but what I really wanted to touch on was how normalized it is to be racist to Asians. In fact, until I got older, I wasn't even able to realize that people were being racist, and even when I did, I wasn't bothered just because of how long I had experienced it. And though I try my best to tell people when they're being racist, I'm just so used to it, that I don't even register it right away.

Another reason why Asian racism is so normalized is because up until recently nobody was paying attention. Most of the Asians I've met are soft-spoken and in most Asian cultures it's frowned upon to bring attention to such big issues, so the issue of racism has just been left alone. As a result, we have this wonderful thing that I experience every day called structural racism. Where even though most people aren't trying to be racist, they are anyway because they act the way that was deemed acceptable growing up.

I just hope that I can do my part in bringing attention to Asian racism with this chapter.

Chapter 3 | Koreans are so Cute ft. Racism

Recently, in the US, the rate of attacks against Asians has increased. Elderly Asian people are being attacked in public streets in big cities and even one elderly Asian has died as a result of such an attack. Yet why is this news not front-page news, or making the headlines?

Unfortunately, I can't give you an answer to that question because I do not know. With all of the publicity the Black Lives Matter movement has received, you would think that the Stop AAPI (Asian American, Pacific Islander) Hate movement would gain just as much. But it hasn't, and I think this is because some people* agree with these aggressors' actions.

*I am not saying or implying that every person agrees with these attacks, what I am stating here is that there is a very small percentage of people who may support these attacks.

I'm here to tell you that the people attacking Asian Americans are wrong.

It sounds redundant, doesn't it? The thought that I have to tell the readers of this book that attacking human beings, spitting in their faces, yelling racial slurs, and telling other people to kill themselves is wrong. I mean, you would think that this would be common logic. Right up there with wearing clothes in public, stopping at a red light, and putting the cereal before the milk. Sadly, it isn't.

I think what is most disappointing to me is that random people feel as if it is Asian people's fault that COVID-19 exists and that it is appropriate for them to attack random Asians, especially the elderly. To every person who has attacked an elderly person unprovoked, just because of their race (or any reason really), I have one word I would like to call them. Cowards.

The people who attacked the Asian elderly most likely did so because they blame us (Asians) for COVID-19, and subsequently, society shutting down. Now, I have news for them. The reason why society shut down is because of people who refused to adhere to health restrictions and stay-at-home orders. Which, surprisingly enough, aren't just Asians.

The other day I watched a video about an Asian woman who stepped forward and spoke about some of the racist remarks she had received just by walking down the street. One lady had screamed at her to 'go back to her country' (she was born and raised in the US) and another had repeatedly called her 'ching-chong' (an Asian slur). Fortunately, I live in a small enough city where this is uncommon, however, that doesn't mean I live in a bubble. I have also received my fair share of racist remarks.

The earliest incident that I can recall is from when I was in Kindergarten. A boy and his friends were making fun of my eyes while repeatedly saying 'ching-chong' and laughing. I didn't understand what was happening. Those kids didn't do that to anyone else, it was just me. I had told the after-school teacher what was happening, and, I will remember this for the rest of my life, that teacher just laughed at me like I was telling a joke, and told me not to be so sensitive. I told my dad later that night and thankfully, he raised hell.

I have a lot of similar experiences, and through all of them I somehow grew up to be a very confident (almost too confident) Asian woman. I grew up learning how to stand up for myself, how to make friends, be outgoing, and most importantly, I learned when it was appropriate to raise hell. Woefully, this is not the case for most Asians.

From what I've seen and been told, Asians are told to suck it up. And of course, there are exceptions, this is just what I've seen. Most Asians I know are hesitant to speak up whenever somebody wrongs them, so it makes sense why most of the Asians I know are surprised by my loud, outgoing personality. In fact, those Asians see it as a part of my 'Americanism'.

On that note, you wouldn't believe how many people have approached me asking if I'm American. Which I am, by the way, born and raised. I've met more random ladies* asking me if I'm American than I've met formally. Pretty ridiculous.

*This is not an attack against women, this is just a descriptive for an experience that I had that I am recalling. It could've been any random person of any gender.

But I feel like I spent a good amount of time talking about that last chapter, so I instead would like to discuss culture. Quick heads up, I have Korean heritage.

As a Korean-American, I try to incorporate as much of my culture as I can into my everyday life, and yes, that includes kimchi. However, one thing that I always notice is that most people tend to assume my culture. Their common thought when they look at me is, 'Oh she's Asian, must be Chinese.'

I kid you not, there have been people who have come up to me and asked if I'm Chinese, or if they're a little more educated, I may have two options; which are more likely than not, Chinese OR Japanese. Before Kpop had really taken off, whenever I had even mentioned Korea, most people would look confused, or make some assumption like, 'Korea must be in China' (Which is NOT true, Korea is an entirely different country).

Now, it's a little better for me when I say that I have Korean culture because most people now recognize that Korea is an actual country. On the downside, I now have to deal with people asking me if I'm into Kpop or know any Korean celebrities, so there's that.

As a kid I used to eat school lunch but, on some days, I would bring my lunch to school. On those days usually what I would pack is rice, some sort of meat like pork or beef, and then occasionally I would put kimchi or dried seaweed.

I personally like both of them [kimchi and dried seaweed] and I think that they are both delicious, but as a kid, it's normal to alienate different things in general. And when I was younger, in Elementary School, everything was different if it wasn't a PB&J sandwich or regular ham and cheese sandwich.

Personally, when the other kids would try to pick on what I had in my lunch I really didn't mind that much because I was and still am very self-assured and confident in who I am, or during the time when I wasn't I just sat by myself. However, more commonly what happens is, when kids bring cultural foods to school, they're humiliated because of it, and they then get embarrassed and tend to shy away from their culture as I know some of my Asian friends have done in the past.

It can hurt as a kid to have people essentially spit on your culture. Trying to be different is difficult as is, but with people who are constantly looking for something different to stomp on, embracing special things like culture becomes 10 times more difficult.

However, I also think that there are two sides to this, as there are at least two sides to any other issue. The opposite side of this issue is when people try to embrace my culture too much.

It sounds odd, right? I mean, you're probably thinking right now "don't you like it when people embrace your culture", and yes, I do. I want people to be accepting. I want people to be kind. But when people take it a step too far and try to utilize my culture in order to make them look good or give off the impression that they're better than a different person/group, I'm not okay with that.

One example I have of this is just going back to school lunches. I mentioned dried seaweed, and when I was a kid when I brought dried seaweed to school the kids would just pretend that it was disgusting, saying things like "icky" and it really hurt me, but I learned to move past that.

Now that I am a high schooler, I watch other students bring dried seaweed to school, usually, the non-Asian students bring dried seaweed or cultural food to school. Surprising right? And then those students who brought that seaweed to school act as if because of that one food they are suddenly Korean, and I'm not okay with that.

I know that makes me sound unsupportive and hypocritical. And I don't mean to come across as a hypocrite but what I'm saying is that there's a line that needs to be drawn and I'm drawing it right now.

It's important that people of different cultures are respected and are kind to one another, but I do not believe that if a person eats or experiences one thing that's part of a different culture it makes that person a part of that culture.

The last sentence was a bit confusing so just to elaborate, I'm okay and I'm comfortable with people I know, people that I'm comfortable with, coming up to me and telling me that they found something in my culture that they like. I love it when that happens. However, I don't like it when a person that I know or person that I don't know comes up to me and pretends that they're [in this case] Korean just because they've done or they've experienced one thing. In fact, I can tell you about one time where this has happened to me.

I had known this person and they had gone over to a friend's house over the break. We'll call them Charlie.

When Charlie went over there, they had apparently had a chance to go to a Korean restaurant. At the Korean restaurant, they had a chance to eat kimchi, which is a staple in Korean culture and food.

That same person had come up to me on the first day back from break and had acted like she was of Korean descent.

Of course, I believed her. I was very excited to learn that somebody that I knew also was of Korean descent and thought that we could bond over that. I later learned that she had absolutely no Korean background or heritage in the slightest and she just made it seem like she was Korean because she had eaten some kimchi and thought that the culture was cute.

That really made me angry because it gave me the impression that my culture is being made into something trivial that anyone can be a part of, and that it's something that is easily dispensed. It felt as if that person was saying that being Korean was not worth the amount of time and effort that my Asian ancestors have put into my culture.

I try to be very flexible about my opinion regarding culture because I realize that everyone grows up in different environments, but certain behaviors are unacceptable, and this book is my way of putting my honest opinion out there.

Though that is not to say that I hate it when people try to experience Korean culture. I love when people take the time to actually learn about the culture and not just pick and choose what they like and don't.

Those people, usually, are very intelligent and observant; they are the people that I would actually be more comfortable with saying that they understand Korean culture.

Adding onto that, I think an important comparison for this, because this is kind of a complicated lesson, is just don't "adopt" other cultures even if you do learn about them and experience them. Even if you take the time to learn about those cultures, that doesn't mean that you have the right to call yourself a part of that heritage. However, that doesn't mean that you can't experience a culture or learn about it.

All this means is just be a little more observant and respectful when discussing other cultures that are not your own. I have learned about Native American culture from Elementary School, and I have never assumed that just because I learned about the culture, because I've experienced some of it, I'm Native American. It's the same idea here.

For those reading this who have never 'adopted' someone else's culture, especially over something trivial, thank you, and clearly, this lesson was not for you. For those who have basic human decency, please just use this chapter to help expand your understanding of the issue of racism towards young people a little more.

Moving onto lighter topics, one thing that makes me very happy and also a little bit upset is the sudden popularity of Kpop. I'm definitely excited about the spread of Korean culture but with that, I didn't realize before the sudden surge of popularity the unintended consequences of it.

There are so many people on the internet nowadays that are very enthusiastic about Kpop, which I understand because I definitely very much enjoy Kpop and I have my own groups and idols that I like, but what is upsetting is when some people try to assume certain things about Korean culture based on Kpop.

On the internet, a lot of international fans* judge regular people by the same standards they judge Kpop groups and idols. And I think what kind of makes me irritated is that they judge everyone by the standards of their Kpop group.

*I am not saying that every international Kpop fan does exactly what I am about to describe. I am only stating this in reference to the people that I have seen on the internet that do this. There is probably only a very small percentage of international fans that do this.

So, every Korean they see, they're judged by that standard and then shamed if they don't meet that standard. Of course, not everyone does it, in fact, probably only a small percentage of them do, that percentage is just very loud with their thoughts. So, it is a bit of a jarring experience going on social media and seeing a Korean being bombarded with comments about why they can't sing or dance, or aren't pretty enough.

Not only that, but the sudden surge of koreaboos is very disgusting as well. Koreaboos are people that are so obsessed with Korean culture that they call themselves Korean and completely discard any of their legitimate culture(s). It's really disgusting to see people on the internet faking Korean heritage just because they think the culture is cute, and as a person with actual Korean heritage it is heartbreaking to see. Just knowing that people don't respect your heritage enough to not do stupid things like that is like a slap in the face.

And with a completely called for transition, I am going to discuss the fact that with the beginning of COVID-19 and the reopening of the entire US, I have received backlash just for being Asian.

Can we talk about that? Do you have any idea how frustrating it would be to be told to get out of your country or to stop spreading the corona virus just because you're Asian?

I personally haven't received much hate, but I have seen people who have and just knowing about it gives me chills because it could so easily be me.

It just gets really irritating, because first of all why are you going up to random teenagers and telling them to get out of their country, like they're literally minors please back away. Second of all, how do you even have the audacity to do that; if you have a problem with Asian teenagers because of their race, get educated and then take it up with the proper authorities or somebody who can fix your problem.

And I understand that people have lost members of their family, and are very sensitive, but it is never okay to push that blame and those feelings onto other people.

To end this chapter, please allow me to air out the rest of my grievances.

What is with the stereotype that all Asians are shy? Where did that even come from?

I understand some may be a little more introverted, but some people just try to walk over me. I'm not a doormat. Those people get very surprised when I speak up and when I talk because I'm Asian.

I've been told that on the outside I look very docile and I look very pleasant to talk to, and I guess combined with my race I seem like a doormat. I actually have to actively start conversations with this aura of 'You cannot walk over me because I'll crush you like a bug' before I can have a decent conversation.

And then some people get surprised but it's not a nice surprise like 'oh okay you're outgoing in a completely unexpected but cool way.' No-No-No-No-No it's an 'oh yeah that's so weird. Are you sure you're not a defect or something that your parents can return' kind of surprised?

I didn't ask to be treated like I'm a disease. All I want is a little human decency, which is surprisingly hard to get. If I cared much about what other people thought, I probably would act more like the stereotype. Thankfully, I don't.

And with that I have aired the rest of my race-related grievances, see you in the next chapter!

Chapter 4 | Act Your Age

"I will act however I want to!"

That is what I would like to say every single time someone tells me to act my age. See, I find this phrase very confusing because what does it mean to act my age? How should a 14-year-old act?

Now, most people probably have some smart-alec answer to my clearly rhetorical question above, but for the sake of word count, let's discuss it.

If I want to have stuffed animals, I'm childish, and if I want to talk about the stock market, I'm trying to be an adult too soon. So, how am I supposed to act? Is there a guidebook or maybe a list that I can look at and follow? If so, where can I buy it? We'll think of the purchase as a long-term investment. Though, I'd rather not buy a new book every year of my life. That seems like it would be a bit of a hassle, and unfortunately, I'm lazy.

As a teenager, I am living on this fine line called 'you're too young to do this but too old to do that'. A wonderful time I'm having let me tell you.

But the one thing that's been especially constant in my life is this glorious idea we as humans like to refer to as age. At some point, some behavior becomes unacceptable, while other types start being expected. However, how are you supposed to make that transition? Easy, in this awkward, acne-filled time frame called your teenage years. So forgive me a bit when I get confused about how I should be acting at my age.

The truth of the matter is whenever someone tells me to 'act my age' I get a bit uncomfortable. I understand that it may just be a reflex to say that phrase whenever a person is acting childish but is it really necessary to say the phrase to other people? Though some may not want to hear it, everyone has different circumstances. EVERYONE. People will act based on their experiences, environment, and instinct. And as most know, teenagers tend to have the worst experiences and instincts. Environment is really more of a tossup.

Now there may be a bit of confusion, so I'm going to elaborate on my previous statement. To be more specific, my statement about how everyone acts based on their experiences, environment, and instinct.

Let's start with experiences. Experience is what is acquired throughout a person's life and is essentially a form of knowledge. Even though experience is knowledge, it's crucially different from what most perceive as 'intelligence'. How so? Knowledge is generally universal, but experience is idiosyncratic. Experience is gained, arguably, by making mistakes and decisions throughout a person's life. To elucidate my previous point, experience is personal because it's based on a person's circumstances, such as the people around them, their physical environment, and even their society's norms.

How does that tie in with teenagers? Easy, we have the worst experiences, arguably of course. But from our perspective, it really seems like we drew the short stick.

First of all, most of us make horrible decisions, which lead to equally as terrible results. As the perfect conclusion to this horrible concoction, we get this wonderful little piece of knowledge the general public likes to refer to as experience. From those experiences, we then choose two different ways to utilize them. Either as a reason to continue living a pathetic life or fuel for the urge to live a better one. Fortunately, that's not the only thing that contributes to our decision-making.

This brings me to my next point, environment. Whether we'd like to admit it or not, people grow up in different environments. Racial privilege does exist, as does prejudice. Those are just some of society's impacts on a person's environment. Let's start with the other people who directly interact with a person. They are also a part of a person's environment. Don't believe me? Can you tell me that parents, teachers, friends, and enemies don't affect how a person acts and matures? Yeah, I didn't think so.

Kids who grow up in wealthier families usually end up making better financial decisions and live easier lives. As I've said before, everyone is different, so it's impossible for everyone to have been affected by the same people. Thus, making it impossible for everyone to mature and develop in the same way. Combined with a person's experience is the need to get reassurance for decisions which usually comes from the people around that person. This is where environment comes in. Even without experience, with a good enough environment, some kids will still be at a complete advantage compared to other kids. That's really just how life is.

So then, what about instinct?

A personal belief of mine is that instinct is not inborn, at least not all of it. I believe that instinct is nurtured by a person's experiences and environment. How does this tie into my previous points? I just discussed how experience and environment differ with every person, so wouldn't it make sense to conclude that instinct is the same? I'll answer for you- it does. I have absolutely no scientific research to back up any of my claims, but as I said at the beginning of this book, everything is based on my own experiences, so also keep in mind I'm not just pulling everything out of my butt.

To continue on this topic of instinct, have you ever wondered why some people make decisions that seem to be grossly irrational? A part of it can be associated with their instinct, which I believe environment heavily impacts. My belief is that instinct is not only part of what a person is born with, but also the knowledge that they receive from their experiences and the people around them. Making instinct a very unique trait.

Now for the finale. How do these three points tie into the age-old statement, 'act your age'? Well, if everyone is influenced by different things, then it wouldn't exactly make any sense for any person in the world to tell another person to 'act their age'. Would it?

If that doesn't work for you, here's a simplified version of why I'm uncomfortable with the phrase 'act your age'.

I am uncomfortable because it's so subjective to the person making the statement. I've met some adults who believe that 14-year-olds should already be working and making money while I've also met adults who believe 14-year-olds shouldn't leave their house unless they're going to school. It is frustrating.

It was the worst for me in middle school because at that age all I really wanted to do was fit in and not stand out. Having all of the expectations of the adults around me heaped onto me did not help at all. You can argue that because of that I was able to develop a stronger mindset, but you can also argue that because of that I sometimes overwork myself and over- and under-estimate my own abilities.

Regarding the idea of subjectiveness, I also believe that an excuse some adults use is that they were a teenager once too, and one thing I don't think most people realize is that you do forget how it feels to be a certain age.

Contrary to popular belief, just because a person may have been a certain age at one point, does not mean that they understand or can relate to younger people; at least to the degree that most people assume. I may have mentioned this before, but times change, and with the current advancements that we have, time is changing rapidly. It is unreasonable to assume that just because you were an age at some point, you can completely relate to someone who is currently that age. Nevertheless, there are certain times where you could relate to someone younger, but that really depends on you and the other person.

I receive this excuse a lot whenever I discuss the difference in times. I mean of course, they [an older person I was conversing with] were a teenager at some point!

How can they be 40 years old now without having been 15 at some point? It's impossible. However, that wasn't what the conversation was about. The conversation was about how society is evolving, not whether or not they were young. Besides, even if I were to take into account how they were a teenager once, that doesn't mean that they can relate to younger people. There are many components of a teenager and all of them change with time. Yes, older people may have experienced hardships, but so do current teenagers, just in a different form.

Some examples would be that currently, teenagers have a lot they need to face such as cyberbullying, stress, the need for acceptance, self-expression, etc. Though kids now are able to be exposed to different cultures and are able to expand their horizons, we are also exposed to more barriers.

Although, I can't completely dismiss the phrase 'act your age' because it is understandable why some adults tell their kids to act their age. Let me tell you, I can remember plenty of times where I've wanted to and told a kid to act their age.

However, I didn't realize until later that, at a certain age, kids know what they're doing. If they act a certain way, there's a reason. The only problem is that age is not set in stone. It differs in every person, and is, unfortunately, the one thing that I cannot provide any comment on, for the pure reason that I have no good advice to give on that subject.

For the people who skipped through this chapter, people are different, so it doesn't make any sense for a person to tell another person to 'act their age'. If you remember anything I've written in this chapter, remember my previous sentence. Trust me, it'll prevent a lot of unnecessary strains in your relationships, especially with the younger people in your life.

Chapter 5 | Let's Talk About Sex

Well, we actually don't. At least, not in schools.

Sex education. The two most dreaded words for a seventh grade teacher to hear (maybe a P.E. coach as well). Fear is a powerful thing, isn't it? So powerful that my seventh-grade teacher "forgot" to teach that part of the curriculum. I'm completely serious. They didn't even go into AIDS or STIs in general. When asked about STIs, I believe they said, and I quote, 'I don't recommend it.' Well, who would have thought?

Now we may think that that is funny, and honestly it was a little. But as I grew older, I realized that I wasn't as educated in certain topics as much as I should've been. Though I grew physically, my mind didn't mature at the same pace.

I definitely realized that once I began high school.

This next story didn't happen to me, because my school is relatively small, but this happened to my friend (her school is about 4.7 times larger than mine). Just a note, we'll call my friend: Beth.

At the time Beth was a freshman in high school. She had gone to the same middle school as me, so she also had a lack of sex education. A couple of months into the school year the school nurse ends up going classroom to classroom explaining, you guessed it, sex. Except, it wasn't a lecture, but more of a giving of condoms. I believe she phrased it as, 'Imagine the Easter bunny with its basket of eggs, except, replace the eggs with condoms.'

Beth was stunned. She had no idea what they were at first. I believe she asked an upperclassman what they were. I envy the balls on her. I would've never been able to do that.

That story essentially summed up my knowledge of sex and any other related topics when I was a freshman. Even when I got to high school, teachers would avoid the entire topic of sex unless it was completely unavoidable. Even then, they'd spend as little time as they could on the topic. It was pretty harsh.

I kind of expected that when I got to high school, I would receive proper education about sex. The worst thing about not being taught properly isn't the embarrassment of having to ask an upperclassman, but the avoidance we get from adults when we ask questions. When students do get the courage to ask an adult a question about their body, more often than not, the adult brushes off the question, or avoids the kid. We understand that they're embarrassed, but adults need to understand that it's a two-way street. Kids are embarrassed to ask the questions. If a child works up the courage to ask an adult a question, they shouldn't be avoided just because they made someone uncomfortable*.

*I use the word uncomfortable liberally in this scenario, but as a disclaimer, if someone makes you uncomfortable in a way that could possibly affect your wellbeing (physical, mental, sexual, or otherwise), then please avoid that person (or report them if it gets serious).

Thankfully, I took Anatomy and Physiology under an amazing teacher who was not afraid to answer any type of question. So, the gaps in my knowledge were eventually filled. Shout out to you Dr. Ellis!

To be completely honest, I'm a little embarrassed writing this chapter. But I'm writing this chapter because I feel like it's an important topic that needs to be discussed.

Most of my knowledge of sex didn't come from my teachers, or the nurse, but actually from my friends. I feel like that's common because that's the way everyone else I know learned about sex. I learned through my network of people [small network]: how to stay safe, social norms, etc. The craziest thing though is the one lesson that I've had repeated to me thousands of times isn't actually any of the things I just mentioned. It has to do with pregnancy.

I've heard the stories, how this girl got pregnant in high school and it ruined her life and so on. I've heard the stories so many times I'm actually terrified of that happening to me. I've heard over and over again, 'don't get pregnant' and 'it'll ruin your life', but no one wants to tell me how to stay safe and actually educate me about sex. I understand the concern, but it would have a much larger impact if I understood the topic you were warning me about. This brings me to my next point.

Did you know that most of the female students I know have been told at least once in their lives to not get pregnant in high school? It's frustrating to be constantly told the same thing while simultaneously having no one be willing to discuss the topic with you.

Sadly, that's the reality for many female and male students. Thankfully, I don't believe that to be the case in my school because of my awesome teacher and the others like her, but many others don't have a teacher like I do. And it's hard to find one, because no one wants to talk about sex.

In addition, there are no easy resources (regardless of what some may say), and rarely are the nurses approachable*, combined with the fact that most students are not educated and they're scared.

*Not due to the nurses' abilities, but mostly due to how embarrassing it can be for the student to approach someone about the topic of sex.

Makes for a pretty hazardous combination if you ask me. That's why sex education is important. It emphasizes the facts and prevents irrational fears and panic. Short-lived embarrassment for lifelong success. Doesn't that sound like a reasonable tradeoff?

Really though, this chapter was more to emphasize the importance of sex education for teens and to show what a lack of education can do to kids from a teenager's point of view.

Chapter 6 | I'm a People Person

I am a people person, I like people (mostly), and classify myself as an extrovert. When I interact with people, I try to make their day brighter and I try to make every single person I meet happy by helping them smile. I don't think most people realize this, but a smile goes a long way. It makes my day better as well as theirs. But I'm not writing this because I expect this information to one day be on a Wheel of Fortune episode, but because I want to share an important message.

As a teenager in my community sometimes it can be hard to be amicable because everyone is just so used to having to expect some kind of catch, and the unfortunate part is that in most cases, they're right to think that. Specifically, though, it's sad for me to see; especially when I interact with people and my actions come across as abrasive or offensive because of the unusual nature of them. I also feel like during this pandemic people have gotten very short-tempered, and I don't really blame them. I understand where they're coming from. A lot of people have lost family and friends to the pandemic and just living during a global pandemic is no walk in the park either; however, I don't feel like that is an excuse to treat people like dirt. As you may be able to see, I have a lot of feelings, but I promise that they'll make sense in a little bit.

I try not to be too blunt because I feel like everyone is pretty sensitive right now. Though it's more like everyone is very sensitive in general now, which should not be an issue, except I want to be able to express my opinion without stepping on anyone's toes. It shouldn't be that difficult, but with how fragile people's egos seem to be, it is. Because of that, sometimes I feel like as an extrovert it's just gotten harder and harder for me to have simple conversations.

I like to say hi to people I've never met in order to make friends, I like interacting and having fun conversations, and I'm that one kid that when you transfer to a new school is the first person that you talk to, that's me! And I feel like people are just very suspicious and untrusting of others, so my natural personality doesn't come through how I intend it to. In fact, I've been told that I come off as loud, annoying, and just overall abrasive in the beginning. Due to that, I tend to have some not-so spectacular interactions and I understand now why some people choose to forgo pleasantries. But interactions make up a large part of who I am, and I don't want to have to change this part of my personality just because of a couple of bad conversations.

Even with this mindset, it continues to become harder every single day when I try to interact with someone and they become extremely defensive over a light remark or they get offended by something little that I say. I try to be very understanding and make it a point to keep in mind that some people get offended by some kinds of certain things that you may not expect. I respect that, but when it gets to a point where they're asking for very unreasonable things, I think that that's a fine line that should be discussed beforehand in order to avoid huge outbursts that most people are seeming to favor nowadays.

These kinds of things definitely do not help me when I'm being my extroverted self, and I know that these things are a pain for all of my introverted friends- who don't even like talking to new people.

But how does this tie into why I think this is such an important topic to discuss and my point of view as a teenager? Before I answer that, I would like to share a couple of stories.

As a kid, and even now, my parents would tell me stories about how they grew up.

It goes without saying that my parents and I grew up in very different environments, but it's a bit more special for my family. My mom grew up in Seoul, South Korea and she attended school her entire childhood, which sounds pretty redundant as most would think it goes without saying, but it's different in different countries where you may have to pay some kind of fee after Elementary School to continue attending school, which at my parents' time you did. Though I believe at the time, in South Korea, the fee was kind of cheap but for very poor families it was difficult for them to send their kids, not because of the fee but because sending their children to school was seen as a less worthy use of time when those families had farms and other things to worry about--but that's a side note and a mouthful.

Anyways my mom grew up being told to focus on her studies and as a result, she was a very successful student and though she definitely made her family proud, her focus wasn't on social interaction. It was on essentially academics, basically, 100% if not 90% or more of the time.

On the other hand, my dad came to the US as a kid and at the time he could not speak English, so as you would expect, he was bullied pretty ruthlessly throughout his academic career. I would say even up to before college. Because of that, my dad's focus wasn't really on social interaction either but more just general survival of high school, not to say that the goal of middle school wasn't also pretty much surviving.

In comparison, I'm growing up surrounded by amazing people like my mom, dad, Godmother, and aunts (shout out to my Gomo who's gracious enough to help me all the time), who place an emphasis on academics, self-worth, and confidence, but not much on social interaction. As such, I think it came as a surprise to my parents and my relatives that I became a very outgoing child.

I like interacting with new people and I love being able to talk (and talk and talk). As a teenager, it's easier for me to be more accepting of that aspect of myself, but when I was younger, growing up I felt like I was a kind of a different breed, which you could definitely say sounds kind of weird.

Essentially, I live in Las Cruces, a very--compared to bigger towns and cities in the US-- small city. In addition to that, I didn't really get the chance to talk to many other Asians because at my elementary/middle school I was essentially one of the only Asians. Due to the small Asian population, my family has to go to a close, much larger city (El Paso, Texas) to actually be able to purchase some authentic Korean groceries and products, and visit restaurants to just have a taste of our heritage (outside of home). There [El Paso] we would meet other Asians.

They were usually very shy and they would try to blend into the conversation and try to not stand out. Like how there are people who lead a conversation and there are people who discuss whatever topic comes up. Then of course there are background people. Most of the other Asians were consistently the ones who played the background people. So, I guess due to all of that, it doesn't ring false that I legitimately thought that I was a fake Asian. I thought I had a defect or something because none of these other Asians had any of these outgoing traits or anything remotely similar to me.

Really, I would say it was up until the third grade that I believed that I was some kind of mutant. Near the end of third grade, I was moved into a fourth-grade class because I wanted to skip a grade, and as you would expect, it didn't go so swell.

Academically I was pretty capable so I wasn't having problems on that front, but I still had my 'identity crisis' I needed to handle and socially I was struggling a little bit. My friends from the grade I had skipped out of didn't want to hang out with me because they thought I left them behind or betrayed them. And the people in the grade I skipped into didn't want to be around me because I was just this annoying underclassman that they've only seen around during after-school care.

As a result, I had to take a step back and reevaluate who I was as a person, and essentially define to myself what my relationships and friendships were with certain people. Essentially, this time was just a time of self-discovery for me and during this time is when I would say I built up most of my self-confidence. Of course, firstly I had to hit my superficial 4th-grade 'rock bottom', but you know what they say: once you hit rock bottom there's nowhere to go but up.

So I picked myself up.

Because of that now I would say that I have some very solid self-confidence, self-esteem, and sense of self. During that time, I think what I needed most was for me to see myself in a position where I could treat myself as a real person and not as a puppet, not as a tool, and definitely not as a sort of defect. I will be forever grateful to my 4th-grade self that she did not give up and just continued to be herself. As a result of her actions, I stopped placing so much weight on myself and the actions of people around me.

That year was when I became much more confident in who I am and started becoming a people person, and to me becoming a people person was one of the best things I did for myself.

To me, being a people person is showing myself every single day that my unique sense of self attracts other people and that I can make friends because I know who I am and I'm willing to act on my ideals. It continuously lets me know that I'm willing to keep my personality and not change it to make myself seem more popular or more normal. And although it's great, it's sometimes hard to do that, even after all of my experiences, because sometimes I feel like people don't want me to be myself or people are just rude in general, and this is where a teenager's perspective comes to play.

I don't know if it's just me, but I feel that most adults want kids to be all the same because it makes them easier to understand. And because of that, when kids stand out it usually, in the beginning, garners a pretty negative reaction.

It could be in the form of subtle disrespect or even general dismissal of certain experiences, and for me, the dismissal of my experiences when I was beginning to find my sense of self. I feel like it's important for me to say this and put my story out there because there are kids right now who are constantly trying to make themselves stand out. Not just for potential colleges, not just for random family reunions that happen every two years, but because they want to improve themselves so that when they look at themselves in the mirror every morning, they're able to see someone that they can be proud of. Someone that they know is uniquely themselves. They can look at themselves in the mirror every single morning and be proud of who they are.

And just by saying that I want to get my message out there and let people know that it's okay to just be yourself, even if it's different from everyone else. I also want to educate people about how there are harmful behaviors that we unconsciously do when something unknown or something uncharacteristic or even just plain new happens. And that is what I am doing with this chapter.

When I was first starting to create my own sense of self and build up my self-esteem, the first reaction I got was pretty neutral. This doesn't sound so bad, but when you react like this to a 3rd or a 4th grader it's pretty harsh, mostly because at this point that kid is trying to create something that the world doesn't have: their own personality.

Then, as that kid, when you get a reaction from people that you're supposed to trust that is not as enthusiastic as you expect, it's pretty heartbreaking. It makes sense that people would react like that though. Growing up I watched the "regular" kids who all seemed to blend together get a lot of praise and positive feedback, and I guess that most people expect kids to act like that.

But, as a child and even now as a teenager, watching those generic kids get treated so well, you feel pressured to act the same way because you want that same amount of attention. However, I want every person reading this book right now to know that it is always better to be yourself. You hear this in movies, books, and even from counselors, but as another kid, I want to share this message. Everything works out in the end, so just keep working hard.

One thing that really helped me when I was becoming who I am, specifically a people person, was that some people along the way very much encouraged me to be who I am and continue on my path. It helped even more that these people were very close to me. They were my parents, my Godmother, and a couple of teachers and principals here and there. They supported me as a person and as someone who was and still is trying to figure themself out.

I can tell you right now that if I didn't get the support that I got as a kid when I was stepping out of my comfort zone, I would not have become a people person. I would probably be a little terrified to talk to people; I'm not going to lie.

Now, I realize that I've talked a lot about becoming more outgoing, and I'd just like to take this moment to say that I'm not saying that people who are introverts have had horrible experiences or that their parents aren't supportive -- what I'm saying is that when I stepped out of my comfort zone, I discovered who I am. People who are introverted may just not be ready to step out of their comfort zone or may have already stepped out and then been burned.

I've seen it happen to my friends and even random teenagers I'm not close to.

It can be hard getting back up when your first time out of your comfort zone doesn't go well. That is why I'm saying this right now, please do not give up when getting out of your shell, and parents, please be supportive. That's why I am writing this book. So that people know that they are not alone with their experiences, and so that parents and family know how they can help.

That said, I'm not saying that you have to be extroverted to be this perfect ideal person. Being introverted may be just as perfect. I just want to encourage other kids like me to take a step out of their comfort zone.

A note for other teenagers: I'm going to tell you right now just take that step, you're going to fight for every inch and there are people out there who will talk to you and support you through it. It might not be right away but trust me, even though it seems like a long step, there will be someone at the end to guide you.

But for the adults, my advice is that you need to be that person to guide that someone who's going to step out. Support means everything. I don't know how much more emphasis I can place on it.

So, I know I've talked a lot about change, and how it can be difficult, but the reason why I've chosen to discuss being a people person specifically is because in society, being extroverted comes with more advantages than being introverted. Not necessarily because one is better than the other but notice how there are plenty of books on how to be more extroverted, and little to none about how to become more introverted. It's because being extroverted is better in our current society. Why?

As my dad always says, 'If you don't ask, the answer is always no.' And I, personally, am very thankful that I am growing up as an extrovert and that I have that advantage. But, what about all of the people, especially teenagers, who aren't extroverted?

Firstly, it's important to keep in mind how some people are extroverted.

I sat down and thought about how and why an extroverted person is extroverted and I came to a conclusion of nature and nurture. I'm a genius, I know (note the sarcasm). I believe that when people are born, they have some qualities they naturally were born with, but I also believe that what the person becomes and how they act may depend more on how they were raised. As you know, this book is focused on teenagers, so I'll start there.

It's unreasonable to expect every teenager to be outgoing or emotionally mature. Exempting special cases, most teenagers still are at a stage in their lives where they are creating their own sense of self. For every failure they may have, most teenagers fall back on something that they'll always have, their inborn nature and instincts. And if, as I said, they're "naturally" introverted, then that is the type of behavior they'll fall back on.

Which shouldn't be an issue, except it is. Remember what I said earlier about society's preferences. It's like a vicious cycle. When a person's advancement out of their metaphorical shell goes wrong in the slightest of ways, they retreat, and then if they don't have a good support system, they retreat further into their shell and people judge them. Then they try to get out of their shell and the cycle repeats.

That's why I felt it was so important to be able to share my struggle with change. I want to show people that change is difficult, and not so pretty, but also rewarding. And I want to emphasize how important it is to support other people, introverted or otherwise, and why I felt the need to discuss why I'm a people person.

I would not be who I am today without my support system. Just due to the change in my personality, my life has already become so much easier, and I want to say thank you to everybody who helped me become who I am. Though this chapter may have been anticlimactic, I chose to write it because it shows how far I've come and may give hope to others in their own journeys with change.

Chapter 6 ½ | Dear Teenagers...and Adults

Man, some people are just so dumb.

It's like, I know that was dumb, you know that was dumb, so why did they do that?

And with that, I'd like to introduce you to the bucket with a hole idea. Personally, I don't believe this is a revolutionary idea, though it may very well be for some people reading this today. Credits to my dad for introducing me to this idea.

Essentially the bucket with a hole theory is this. If you try to fill a bucket with a hole up with water, what's going to happen? Easy, it's going to leak. Now, what if you take the bucket to the movie theater and try to fill it up there? It's still going to leak. Alright, then what if you take the bucket to a different country then, fill it up there. The bucket will still leak.

Fine then, let's disregard location. What if we paint this bucket purple? Even after painting the bucket purple, the bucket will still leak. The fact of the matter is that the problem isn't the location nor the appearance of the bucket. The problem is the bucket itself. And the same exact principle applies to people.

As a teenager, I've had my fair share of moments where I've met people and immediately clicked with them, but some people you meet are just kind of off. Maybe it's behavior-wise, and they act like a brat. Or maybe they constantly cause problems everywhere they go.

Whatever it is, wherever you put these people they just cause trouble.

Usually, this is not a problem. Those people are in charge of their own lives, just move along. The problem is when those people are one of your friends. See, my least favorite part of irrationality is that it can develop. I have had some friends that were perfectly fun and fine one year, and when we come back from a long break, BOOM, we have an arrogant brat.

So then, of course, you want to help your friend. It's a natural reaction and I have had this exact same experience more than once.

First, you try talking. Doesn't work – plan B.

Plan B is an intervention. That doesn't work either.

Eventually, you do so much, and you notice that nothing changes. So, you give up.

I always used to feel horrible when this happened because 'what if I had done something different?'. But I'm here to tell you, do not feel bad. Your friend just turned into a bucket with a hole. At that point, they are going through something and the only person who can truly help them are themselves.

This mini-chapter wasn't anything special, but it captures the lesson of the bucket with a hole. Though very minor, size-wise, this lesson has helped me be more accepting and I thought that it would help others too.

So, the next time your toxic friend tries reaching out, or that toxic coworker snarks at you, try to remember the bucket with a hole idea. It may help.

-Lauren

Chapter 7 | The Giving Tree

The first time I read *The Giving Tree* by Shel Silverstein I was 7 years old. I was in kindergarten and the daycare I went to had a system where we would receive points for the number of books we read. It just so happened that I picked The Giving Tree in my quest to gather points.

The next time I read *The Giving Tree* I was in third grade, and even though it was the exact same book, it seemed different somehow. It was like there was a new message that I had just uncovered and decoded. I dismissed the thought and continued reading.

The most recent time I can remember reading *The Giving Tree* is in 7th grade. The thought running through my mind was, 'there is something really odd about this book because every time I read it, it seems like it is an entirely different story'. So, I did what any other curious kid would do and I asked my dad to explain to me why it is that every time I read this book it seems like a different story.

He told me that when you read any book there's always a lesson, *The Giving Tree* just so happens to have one of the best ones. Of course, I'm curious and a little irritated so I push for a more specific answer. Why is this story so different?

The lesson *The Giving Tree* is trying to show is not a lesson but an experience. The reason why this story seems to change with time is because your perspective when reading that book changes with time. When I read that book as a child, I saw it as a fun little story. But as I grew older, I saw it as a friend helping another, and eventually when I grow older, I'll read it as a parent with their child.

This type of lesson was new to me because in school I learned all about books that were trying to teach me patience and other virtuous things, but this book had a lesson that I had never seen before. I had never even heard of a lesson that changed with time. This was an entirely new concept for me and to be frank about the matter, I had a hard time wrapping my head around this idea.

But as I've grown older and matured, I've seen that same-exact time-changing process happen over and over again. The same lessons, except that they seem to change as the person being taught ages. That's what I'd like to discuss in this chapter: how lessons change with time and how to overcome that age-gap with advice from a teenager.

The first concept I'd like to discuss is how lessons age throughout generations.

I've noticed, as a teenager, a lot of parents and grandparents try to pass on lessons, which is admirable especially when most of them have to do with traits such as being patient and respectful to others. But what would also have to be noted is that with time, the delivery of these lessons tends to get a bit outdated.

Society is ever-changing, meaning that there's going to be a lack of connection between generations, whether it's person-to-person, person-to-society, or even society-to-society. And with that loss of connection, when a lesson is passed on from generation to generation, or from parent to child, it loses some of its impact.

Even if these lessons are important or can positively impact someone's life, if you can't have someone actually be willing to learn whatever's being taught and implement it into their life, the lessons really are of no use. For instance, teenagers now are very attached to their phones. The common misconception of many adults [not all] is that we're attached to our phones because we're superficial and don't realize the importance of talking with others in person. This is wrong.

Many kids rely on their phones to get out of their shells and make friends. Of course, online safety is extremely important, however, this is today's approach to the problem of how to create friends. It is not possible or safe for kids to make friends like how the older generation did: by going outside and talking to random strangers. Today, people are more aware of how reckless and dangerous that behavior can be and so as a result our behavior has changed. But that also means that it can be hard for older people to understand why we act like how we do. Because of changes like this, it's much harder for older people to communicate with younger people and vice-versa.

In fact, it only makes it harder to encourage whoever you're trying to teach to implement your lessons into their life if they can't relate to what you're saying or the times you're referencing. I know it sounds kind of crazy but hear me out. You're probably thinking right now "but that doesn't make any sense... they're trying to help them so wouldn't they want them to take their advice" and yes, you would think that but most teenagers I know (and I will admit sometimes I do this as well) will completely underestimate your advice and the weight of your words. Because, let's be honest, as teenagers we all think that we know more than you. We win one argument and all the sudden we know everything about the world, that's really the thought process in our brains.

That said, I think something that is very important, especially for parents or people who are trying to help raise a child, is that they're able to connect; that they're able to establish a connection between them and this younger person. I know that as a teenager it's much easier for me to take an adult more seriously when I know that they're able to relate to me. And it sounds kind of off because you would think that I would be more respectful towards adults who show that they've lived successfully and that they have more experience, but that's really not true.

It already goes without saying that most adults have more experience than us (teenagers) but when an adult puts in the effort to make what they're saying relatable, it shows me that they care and it forces me to give a little more respect to that person. That is some of the best advice I can give as a teenager. Even so, nobody in this world is a psychic and some people may need a little more help relating to their kids (or any kids) so here are my top tips for relating to your kids.

My number one tip for creating a connection and getting more respect from teenagers unconsciously is to communicate. When I say communicate, I don't mean confront your kids and make them tell you about all their deepest darkest secrets. No!

What I'm saying is show your kids that you're willing to listen. You want to be able to be a person that a teenager or any younger person can feel comfortable going to and talking to. Personally, I find that not many people are willing to just openly communicate. Instead of having open discussions, everything is 'he said, she said'. And it's a little discouraging from the teenager's side because it seems like you are not listening to me.

To tell the truth, anything you force is not going to be effective, it's only going to build mistrust and, in the end, lose you respect. I have had school counselors that have tried to push kids to talk about what they're struggling with (mental or societal problems) and I've seen the distrust between the students and counselors build up. Even as a third party it was clear to me to see how the little relationship that they may have had gets stretched and stretched until one day it snaps, just like a rubber band that's been pulled too far.

Once you are patient enough to just listen and you've continuously shown whoever you're trying to support that you're there, most kids will talk to you and they will communicate with you. At this point, contribute to the conversation, don't control it. It never fails to boggle me how some people just try to make the conversation all about them. If you want a healthy relationship, you need to give. It's give and take, not take and give – just like a vending machine.

My second tip for creating that connection is to be in control of yourself, and this tip is all for whoever is reading right now. Whereas the first tip is somewhat dependent on a relationship, this one is about yourself and how mentally you're able to support another person. This tip is tied directly with the first however it's a little different.

In the first tip I mentioned how important it is to communicate, however, what I didn't go into was how when you start trying to reach out, the person you're trying to communicate with may not want to communicate with you back. And, not to call anyone out, that means that you probably already messed up somewhere.

I can guarantee you, if that happens, one of the first initial feelings you'll get when they react in a negative way is frustration and anger. But before you get angry, before you get frustrated, the questions I always ask are why and who am I angry at. If your answer is your kid, there are only two reasons why I think this could be: 1) a very significant reason which would also require communication to solve, or 2) you're taking out your feelings on a child.

When you take out your feelings on your kid, you might as well be using us as your free punching bag. I don't think some people realize how tiring and frustrating it can be to be treated like a metaphorical emotional punching bag. See, kids are just kids, you can't subject them to those kinds of emotions. Adults? No, that would be too embarrassing. So what are we left with? Teenagers!

Now, I'm not berating or putting anyone down for having strong and overwhelming feelings because I've felt them many times myself. But if you cannot control your feelings, or don't have a healthy (or any) stress reliever, just take care of yourself first. Trust me, we (teenagers) can tell if you're actually putting 100% of yourself into our relationship, and I think it goes without saying that you can't do that if you're not in control of yourself.

My last tip is to know yourself. This one goes hand in hand with the last tip.

Before you even try to support another person, it's important that you know who you are. If you cannot take care of yourself, you cannot take care of another person.

Honestly, just saying this is pretty easy, but executing it is a lot more difficult. I've even had my fair share of troubles with this.

When I was younger, I had a very hard time making friends, which left me as a very vulnerable kid to manipulative other kids. In the fourth grade, I had a pretty rough time transitioning because I had just skipped into the class. I had no friends and it was a very rough time for me.

During this time, one girl decided to be friends with me. I'm telling you right now, I was so grateful to this girl that I wanted to support her and do everything I could for her. When we reached Middle School, this girl changed, and not for the better, but I just continued wanting to support her. I always stood by her side and it did burn me a couple of times.

Looking back on that relationship I know that the reason why I was dragged along for so long was because when I was at a time in my life when I was doubting myself, somebody formed a connection with me that I became dependent on, and so I learned to support that somebody when I couldn't even support myself.

I'm not sure if this girl did it on purpose because even with everything that I've been dragged through, she never really showed any malicious feelings toward me. It was like I was collateral damage. And the reason why I'm including this tip is because if you don't know yourself you can make somebody else collateral damage, and nobody wants that.

That is why it is so important to know yourself. If you aren't ready to commit yourself to a relationship, don't go charging in headfirst. In all of my experience (which isn't a lot), it never ends well.

Moving onto a slightly happier note, let's discuss giving. Recently my dad, if you couldn't tell I really like my dad, sat me down to talk about this new concept. Except it wasn't really a new concept-- it's been around for ages-- it was just a new concept for me. He called it the vending machine lesson.

Here's how the lesson went.

My dad asked me how vending machines work. I tell him you put in money, then you press a button and get the product that you paid for, essentially. At that moment I was thinking that my dad may slightly be an idiot, but it's all good because there was actually a place he was going with this. Then, of course, my dad answers with some philosophical remark and says,' so doesn't it make sense that it's the same in life'. The answer is yes, and I'm going to tell you why, with a teenager twist.

Through my dad's surprisingly straightforward example he was trying to teach me one lesson; which was you must give before you take, it's give and take not take and give.

What I mean by 'it's give and take and not the other way around' is that you need to give before you can receive--just like a vending machine. No vending machine will just let you take whatever you want from it and then come back later and pay them. No. You have to put in money first and then you get what you want. And it's kind of the same with life, you give and then you receive. Of course, there are some complications that may give different results that can come up but essentially, it's the same idea down to its core.

For teenagers, or at least for me, when I think of this lesson, I'm a little bamboozled. If you think of it from a really simple standpoint, what's the difference between give and take and take and give?

They're practically the same thing and there's not really much of a difference. My thought process was that give and take is like the commutative property, and I could not be more wrong.

My personal belief is that humans are selfish creatures, especially kids and teenagers. This may or may not have also been proven by psychologists and scientists but even so I still fully believe this.

As you get older the people around you teach you how to act and what is acceptable, but when you're young naturally all we want to talk about is me me me. And as a teenager that's when we're making that transition from becoming that selfish child to becoming a more mature person. So, how does this tie in with the vending machine lesson? I'm getting to that.

Of course, there are bumps in the road and that's when we want to be like "okay you do this for me and then I'll help you", which is not how life works at all. As an adult it may be pretty obvious; you have to do someone a favor before they do you a favor. But as a teenager, we're thinking as rationally as we can. The unfortunate part is that sometimes our rationality is different from yours. And I know this is frustrating for a lot of people to hear because it's easy to always want to put yourself first. However, by placing others first, you actually get more out of your relationships. You form stronger bonds, by essentially putting yourself out there first. Still regarding common sense, I found that it really pays off being the first to reach out.

And for the adults who may not have understood my lesson, what I'm saying is that before you receive you need to be able to give just like the vending machine. If you want to earn someone's trust you need to give yours first. If you want a favor from someone you need to do them a favor first. And sometimes you can't force it. Sometimes you give and you give and give and you get nothing back. That's what we call a broken vending machine. Other times you'd only give a dollar and get nothing and then the person behind you puts in a dollar and they get two things. Or sometimes you put in something and expect to get out one thing and you get two things. There are so many variations with the lesson, but at its core, it is the same one, you need to give before you receive.

Thank you to my dad for this lesson and I hope that all the advice in this chapter was helpful.

Chapter 8 | Confidence - A Saga

I am confident.

The first time I said this sentence it was almost a wish. A tentative, yet hopeful wish. Now when I say this, it's a fact. Indisputable and true in every aspect. However, this is not the case for most teenagers. Let me explain why.

Most of the teenagers I've met are in a place where they're first starting to discover who they are. I don't know if this is fortunate or unfortunate but early on, I had the chance to cement the foundation of who I am which has helped me become more confident in myself.

Though that's not to say I was always confident. When I was younger there was always something that I wanted to change about myself; I wanted to be prettier, smarter, skinnier, but at some point, I just learned to love myself. For most teenagers, that's not the case because when they look in the mirror they see a flawed version of themselves. This has happened to me. Sometimes it feels like the longer I look the more flaws I find. I would assume most if not every teenager has had that same experience.

It's hard to cope with. But one special experience that comes with being a teenager is learning to discover who you are.

Most adults already know who they are, or at least have some idea, and I know that at some point some adults start to remember less and less about *how* they got to where they are and focus more on their end result (in terms of self-discovery).

That isn't bad per se but when we're talking in terms of teenagers it can be harmful. When we forget the process of whatever we do, we value it less, and in relation to what I am saying, that means that everything that we go through as teenagers at some point we're just going to see some kids playing around instead of young adults going through a journey of self-discovery because we've already gone through the process.

Once you've gone through the process of self-discovery it seems a lot easier to then watch other people go through the same thing, especially younger people. Some adults seem to think that younger people are just less intelligent or something equally as insulting. It's frustrating because as teenagers we watch this kind of reaction and it wears us down. I've seen teenagers worn down to such a point where they don't even want to become a unique person; they just want to do everything they can to fulfill the expectations of the people around them and when they can't meet the expectations they eventually fall apart.

This is a huge reason why I think it's really important to acknowledge the struggles that teenagers are going through, especially in terms of creating their own sense of self. I also believe that confidence plays a large part in this. Once you know who you are, you become more confident in yourself. It just goes to show that if you know who you are and where you stand, confidence is just an extension of yourself.

So as long as you know yourself, you will be more confident. And I think that's also another reason why you don't see a lot of teenagers who are confident, because they don't know who they are yet. How can you create an extension of something if you don't even know what that something is?

As someone who's in the middle (someone who's a teenager and also confident), it's hard for me to watch some people look down on teenagers because they're not confident. I know how difficult it is to be confident and to understand yourself, and watching other people degrade some teenagers' journeys into self-discovery is hard.

It is not like I am introducing brand new topics. I am not a genius, but I have something that a lot of people don't right now, and that's time. With that time, I can see more and understand more. But one thing that I can see the best right now because of my age is when understanding and compassion are lost in age gaps. I, and probably every other teenager, know when we are being brushed off because of our age. I know when my confidence is being stomped on because it looks 'childish' to adults. But sometimes people can't see what they're doing, so I'm hoping this book can be a window into our point of view.

Another thing that can be and is very frustrating for teenagers is sometimes it feels like parents want us to grow up fast-- to create our own personality and then build off of that in a matter of days-- but I don't think most people realize that it takes a solid foundation to do that. Every person goes through the same experience where they have to try to create who they are, but at some point, you start forgetting how hard it was just because it's been so long. Also, when you sometimes don't meet certain expectations, as a teenager, it's hard because you just want to impress your parents, teachers, and/or the people around you.

I know, because I've felt like that multiple times. It's like a giant burden has been placed on your shoulders by the people who are supposed to be helping you carry it. But, what helps and has helped me is knowing myself, and with that becoming confident in myself. With confidence, I can say that I have a solid foundation, and I can control my life and the pace of it. I feel free because I know myself and am genuinely confident as a result. And I'm not saying that to come off as standoffish or even arrogant. I am saying this because it has just changed my life. That is why having confidence is so important to me, and I want to be able to share this amazing feeling with other people.

The problem is, I think sometimes it can be very uncomfortable to sit down and discuss confidence. I know most people worry about trying not to cross the line between being confident and being arrogant, but what I firmly believe is that you can go from being arrogant to confident, but if you're not confident in yourself and your abilities there's no way that you can improve yourself- meaning there's no way you can be arrogant. I found that if you're always looking to change something about yourself and are never satisfied, you cannot create a foundation to build your sense of self on. Now, I could always illustrate this idea with a hypothetical situation, but I feel as if it's better to share my story with confidence. After all, this is partly a book about me.

When I was a little kid, I loved myself. I just loved looking in the mirror and overall, I was pretty happy with who I was. But at some point, that started to change. When I looked in the mirror, I wasn't seeing a girl who was happy, I was seeing a girl who was missing a lot of things: wasn't as pretty as she could have been, or as tall as any of the other girls, and then at some point, I hated looking in the mirror. It was like some part of me didn't want to be me anymore and that same part was ashamed to be me. At that point, I was not confident and it was hard for me to build up confidence because I didn't know who I was and I didn't like what I was seeing.

This kind of experience is common for teenagers although the intensity of it may vary. Though something special about my experience was that my honeymoon phase with myself started and finished a lot earlier than my peers—fourth grade to be exact.

In fourth grade, I skipped a grade. It was near the end of the year when I transferred from my third-grade class to this fourth-grade one. With the strangely timed transition, it's safe to say that I did not have any friends. The school I went to was really small, so small that there was only one fourth-grade class and one third-grade class. The fourth graders knew who I was, and that meant that they knew that I was a third-grader, and they didn't want to hang out with me because no older kids want to hang out with younger kids. Fair.

The kids from my grade felt betrayed that I had left so I didn't have any friends in that grade either. At this point, most kids would probably say that this was the moment where their confidence dropped, and then they became self-conscious for the rest of their life. I was almost one of those kids. However, at some crucial moment, there was a voice in the back of my head that just kept screaming at me, "If you give up now what are you going to do when the next big challenge comes around? If you give up now what does that say about your character?".

I was ashamed of the answers that were coming to mind and I knew that if I didn't step up, I would not be able to look myself in the eye ever again. I knew I would never be able to smile genuinely and tell myself and others that I liked who I was. So, I stood up and fought for myself.

I fought for myself the rest of that year and became a people person through it all. I made plenty of friends and my middle school years were full of laughter. I fell into a healthy truce with my mind up until the beginning of my freshman year of high school.

I had gone to the same school from Kindergarten to 8th grade, and I was terrified to go to high school. This is when all of those little insecurities started to pop back up. What if nobody likes me? What if I don't make any friends? What if I'm not smart enough? And then, after the first week, I just took a deep breath. I was doing fine in my classes and I had plenty of friends.

After going through such a similar experience earlier in my life, it was so much easier for me to assure myself. After that, I'm not exactly sure what specifically changed, but I know that I changed for the better. I became more self-assured, and at that point, I knew for sure that I was confident.

These are major reasons why I am so confident today. They were times of self-reflection and they allowed me to discover who I was. Of course, during the process, I had some ups and downs (like my experience with lack of friends in Chapter 8) but I was able to get to where I needed to be.

And though my experience didn't seem like much, it made me who I am today.

Most teenagers have similar experiences (usually in middle or high school) and that's why some of them aren't confident. In fact, that is normal! It took me over 3 years to get to where I am now, it makes sense that people are still struggling. They're still trying to figure out who they are and if we expect results from people who haven't even finished the process yet, that makes us the unreasonable ones.

On that note, now I'm at high school and unfortunately, I've seen a lot of people who put on fake smiles. The second you get close to them you realize just how insecure they are, which is not a testament to their inner strength, but it just means that at some point or another they or someone else failed themself. Failure comes when a person isn't able to continue with their journey of self-discovery because of themself and/or if someone else sabotaged it.

As for the people who are confident, teenagers especially, they are because of some kind of past experience like mine. They went through some kind of experience and came out stronger, which is great but can also mean that they may be independent even overly so.

But what is more common are teenagers who are not confident. It makes sense, as most people generally try to create their own personality in middle or high school. And as I've said many times before, confidence is an extension of yourself. This really explains why a lot of teenagers aren't confident. It's not because they're cowardly or weak, but because they're regular kids. And though I want to imply that confidence is an independent journey, it isn't. Yes, a large part of building a sense of self is based on the individual, but the people around that person play a huge role as well. This is where most adults come in.

My number one advice to help build confidence is to communicate, and I know I've said this a lot, but when you talk to your kids or any kids you know, you show them that they have someone in their corner. Which, to an adult, may seem like it isn't really doing much, but as a teenager it brings relief.

I know this sounds ridiculous, but also communicate with yourself. Using a journal or even just talking in the mirror is a great way to build up self-worth and honestly, I find it a great way to just release all of your pent-up feelings.

Just keep in mind nobody is perfect, and there will always be issues, especially with confidence. So, just stick along for the ride. Trust me, it's worth it.

* * *

BONUS:

Confidence can also be built up by acquiring new skills. Sure, it may be hard in the beginning, but it definitely pays off! Here's my current work in progress:

On February 19th, 2021, I had my first driving lesson.

The acceleration pedal is terrifying and I'm completely sure I have developed a temporary phobia of driving.

I was scared because it was my first time behind the wheel, but guess who was in my passenger seat to encourage me? No one, my dad was in the seat. I'm just joking, but if I'm being honest, I'm pretty sure he was scared too.

Let me just walk you through what happened.

I was just--attempting-- to drive in the mall parking lot when my dad and I discovered that I cannot drive in a straight line. I've been told that the easiest thing to do when driving is to go straight. When I drove, I apparently liked to think of 'straight' as a relative idea. It's not.

Adding that to the fact that I just realized that driving a car is not similar to driving a go-cart and that I almost ran into the same light pole 5 times, you get a pretty accurate image of my driving skills. To top it off, I almost hit the curb 7 times when trying to turn. Why am I close enough to any foliage or sidewalk to hit a curb? That's the result of another disaster.

The person I felt bad for the most was my dad. I mean, I was pretty terrified too, I'm not going to lie, but my dad willingly got into a minivan with a 14-year-old behind the wheel.

Of course, my dad tried to be relaxed and tried to play off his panic, but it was clear as day that he was never going to get in a car with me again. Ha! Joke's on him. My mom doesn't want to teach me either.

But I'm hoping that sometime in the future I'll become a better driver and be more confident in my driving skills.

Chapter 9 | Santa's Broke

When I was in elementary school, the Girl Scouts tried to recruit me. The exact words that I had told the troop leader were, "My daddy told me that Girl Scouts is a scam".

Suffice to say, I was never invited back. Such a shame. And surprisingly enough, no girl scout from that point on ever tried to recruit me. It was like the troop leader made it a point to tell the incoming girl scouts, 'not that girl'. And truth be told, I find that hilarious.

But you're probably wondering what Girl Scouts has anything to do with Santa's current state of financial affairs. Easy! I was also the first person in my grade level to learn that Santa wasn't real (don't try to fight me on this, he isn't real). And since I was such a delightful (read: dreadful) child, I decided that it was my responsibility to inform the other children of my grade. I remember the day, like it was 8 years ago (as it was 8 years ago).

It was a wonderfully cool, cloudy day and my Kindergarten class was working on a Christmas craft to bring home to our parents. All of a sudden, one kid started to throw a fit and the teacher told the class to behave or else Santa would not bring any gifts to their homes. Then Kindergarten me decided to speak up and tell the class, "Santa isn't real". I don't remember exactly what happened after that, but what I do vividly remember is that there was screaming, crying, and some vague sounds of betrayal in the background which I'm assuming came from the children, not from the staff members who were trying to control the crying children.

However, before I learned about the truth of Santa, I was just like any other kid. And like most other kids, I used to always ask for things. My dad's solution? Tell his children that Santa was broke. Usually after that, we would, my dad and I and sometimes my siblings, engage in a very time-wasting, unproductive argument about the state of Santa's affairs.

While all of those were entertaining stories, they don't really seem to have anything to do with life from a teenager's perspective, but in reality, they do. I think that when a person is growing up a very important part of that process is their childhood and their early memories, even something as simple as the TV shows they watched as children.

In this chapter, I'm going to be discussing some of the impact my childhood has had on me. Don't worry it's nothing gruesome. I had a very pleasant childhood and actually, I was quite spoiled, in fact, looking back on it I was probably a terrible child, but that's a story for another time.

Moving back on topic, one of my favorite things to do as a kid was watch TV. I watched tons of different shows: ones with superheroes, amusement parks, princesses, and of course the iconic show with a talking sponge that I'm not going to mention due to copyright. By watching these shows I learned a couple of very important ideas and traits, the first of which is Family Matters. I also learned the power of hard work and determination. Just for funsies, I also learned how to twirl like a princess, not to brag or anything.

Now when I say that watching stuff on TV taught me new things, what I'm saying isn't exactly anything new; I mean people have known this for ages, however, what I don't think people actively realize is that you not only learn ideals and traits and qualities from TV shows that you watch as a kid but you also learn expectations.

Things that are acceptable in public and in general and you also learn how to judge yourself. I can confidently say that I have not judged myself by the standards of a child show for a couple of years now, please keep in mind that I'm very young, but I cannot say that I have not judged myself from the TV shows that I watch now.

Sometimes when I'm feeling very down, I watch these shows and automatically assume that if I'm not exactly like the main character I'm going to be alienated and not going to have any friends and just be uncomfortable for the entirety of my high school career. This is pretty ridiculous, but sometimes I just seem to spiral into this sort of panic mode. It's much easier for me to want to feel a part of a group, rather than stand out.

As a kid, it is very important to us that we are accepted. It means more for us to be able to be in the "In Crowd" rather than be our unique selves. And our perception of what is 'in' is directly affected by our experiences as a kid.

Seeing on TV the popular girl being pretty, skinny, and smart makes kids (or at least child me) want to be the same. It's almost like an urge and this feeling is not easy to control, although it's perfectly natural. Once you have this feeling, it can be hard to just accept who you are, because you want to be someone else.

But it is so important to be accepting of who you are because everyone is their own special person. If we spend so much time trying to change ourselves, we won't have enough time left to improve ourselves. And yes, change is different from improvements. You can only improve what you have, and if you can't even accept yourself, then you cannot improve.

The right childhood experiences can set a person up for success from the beginning. By encouraging self-love and confidence in the beginning, kids grow up to be more self-assured. But, if you go a different route and surround a child with sources that make them question who they are and doubt themselves, the self-doubt will linger for the rest of their lives. That is why childhood experiences are so important. They make a difference by creating a baseline.

On a less serious note, I'd like to go back to the Santa story. I told this story for two main reasons: the first is it's funny, and the second is I feel like this is a great example of what I was talking about before about how our childhood experiences affect us.

When I was in kindergarten or maybe around that age, I learned that Santa Claus was not real. Don't feel bad for me, thinking about how my childhood ended early because of this, because it was really truly my fault that I discovered that Santa wasn't real. Kindergarten me wanted to stay up Christmas night and wait for Santa and unlike most other children who fall asleep around the time that parents get up at night and put the presents under the Christmas tree, I actually was able to stay up and I don't know if it was good or bad.

Anyways, that's when I discovered that Santa Claus equals my parents. It was quite a shock. I was very shocked. I would like to say my parents and I had a very long conversation after that confrontation and that we just moved past it like normal people, but no. After I caught them in the act of putting presents under the tree, I genuinely believed that I was asleep so I did a 180, went back to my room, and went to sleep, and when I woke up, I literally acted as nothing had happened. Of course, a couple of days later I talked to my dad and asked him if he's really Santa Claus, and surprisingly enough he replied "no, Santa Claus doesn't exist" and then my mind is blown. After that you know the rest, I scarred my kindergarten class as children and I also made my kindergarten teachers very frustrated, so I'm pretty proud of that.

As to what I was saying before, this story summarizes what is one of the most vivid memories I have to date. Because of this I always question whatever facts or information that is provided to me is accurate. And it has done me much good in the past and still is, so I'm very grateful for that. But what it also has taught me is that there are some people who do not want to grow up and honestly, I don't blame them. I'm very happy being a freeloader. I do absolutely nothing and get hot showers, a warm bed to sleep in, a roof over my head, constant support, so essentially a lot.

You may not think that it's such a big deal that as a kid I knew that Santa Claus was not real but it was a big deal to me, because when I compare myself, because yes, we love comparisons here, to my peers especially those who still believe in Santa Claus I see this different way of thinking. I'm not going to say maturity because I know people who still believe in Santa Claus who are very mature and are very responsible so I feel like the word mature is not a good word to use in these circumstances.

Those people who still believe in Santa Claus, based on my personal experience, are much more creative than I am and they seem to have the wildest imaginations. The only problem is that they have a very hard time grasping onto reality. They're the people who have the dreams of being number one in the world in whatever field they're interested in and then they don't choose to put in hard work just because they genuinely believe that fate or destiny is going to lead them to that dream.

Honestly, I'm fine with those people. I am glad that they are shooting for the stars, but the thing is that they're very unreasonable people as well. Some refuse to budge on their beliefs or compromise, so it can be a bit difficult trying to communicate with them.

On that note, I'm not saying that not telling your kids Santa Claus exists is going to ruin your kids' lives. I think that fun traditions like that make life more interesting and are great for kids growing up. But, as a teenager watching other teenagers still believe in things like that, I feel like there is a time where if your kid hasn't figured out that Santa Claus doesn't exist yet, you should tell them. I believe that at some point every person needs to be able to mature a little. It just comes with growing up.

So then, what about the kids who learned early on that Santa Claus does not exist?

Well, on the other side of the spectrum, we have the type of kids who were like me. The ones who made other fellow children cry since kindergarten. Those are the kids that I see who are more logical. They're much more realistic; you never really see them with the big dreams. They're the ones who want to be doctors, lawyers, and prosecutors. They tend to have a great grasp on reality, and they know what they're doing, why they're doing it, and how they're going to do whatever they're going to do.

But those people are very direct and rigid about what they believe in and where their work is going. Though they are definitely the ones who are willing to put a lot of effort into what they believe in, if whatever they're doing starts to fail or looks like it isn't going to succeed these people are also one of the first people to jump ship.

You could argue that these people are better because they know where their priorities are and they know how to get things done. But you could also say that they're the type of people you might not want on your team because they're not willing to stick around for the long run. So, like most things in life, there's a special balance between logical and creative.

This was just one example of how childhood experiences can impact kids. There are hundreds of others out there. One that immediately comes to mind: the Tooth Fairy. However, there is no need to be too controlling with a child's experiences because childhood is just one part of a person's life that affects them.

Though I made my last example very simple, nothing in life works the same. Telling (or not) your kid about the truth of Santa is not going to shape their lives. It'll be just one in the hundreds of thousands of experiences they will have. Even as a teenager, some of the things that have affected me the most are the fun things that happened when I was a kid or even things that happened just recently.

So many different traits can develop in kids from so many different places.

Even though every parent wants their child to fall in between imaginative and logical while also being realistic, I think it's also important to remember that every person grows up differently regardless of whether they have the same parents. There is no perfect way to raise a child because every child is different. Even if two kids grew up in the same exact school, environment, and town, they're going to grow up to be different people. Even identical twins are different.

As a child who has had these experiences growing up in the present, having different beliefs and choosing what to base your beliefs on is important. It gives a person--a teenager or kid-- their very first feeling of what's it like being in control of themselves even if they're not actively aware that they're choosing what to believe or choosing how to think for themselves. It's something that's very important. Giving children the chance to choose their own choices based on their experiences.

So, I guess the question now is when is the best time to tell my child the truth (about anything really-including Santa), and then have them choose for themselves? And really, I can't answer that, because every person matures at a different pace and every person grows at different rates. But as a teenager, it can be confusing, and my advice would be do not worry.

My advice for teenagers: you are your own person, you'll know when you're ready.

My advice for parents: good luck!

Before I end this chapter, I'd like to touch base on that girl scout story. Of course, it was humorous and all, and I legitimately believe that I am shadowbanned from Girl Scouts, but another thing that I think is important too is to show kids the reality of what's going on. This ties in directly with that mental maturity concept (where you believe you are capable of taking a step into reality).

I think it's very important that the people around teenagers are able to help guide teenagers before they came to self-realization; it may help them adjust to the reality of a situation. In the case of the Girl Scout cookies, I would say the fault there's a little on my dad because I was definitely not ready to hear about how Girl Scout cookies are a scam (which they are by the way feel free to argue with me), but other than that I would say that my parents did a fantastic job raising me and leading me not only as my parents but as my role models and as people I know that I can trust. I do believe that every child should have a person like that by their side growing up - someone who will give them their experiences or at least lead them through them when they're younger. I have my parents, my Godmother, and I have a lot of other amazing people by my side that I could not be more grateful for.

All of those people have helped lead me through life and introduce me to reality piece by piece. If you're a parent reading this, I encourage you to do the same.

Chapter 10 | Streaking - 0/10 Wouldn't Recommend

To begin (for the last time), we're going to start with the one thing every person has either hated or loved, social norms. If you don't know what social norms are, they are things that are seen as normal or standard by the general public. For example, when you want to learn information about another person (i.e. their name) you offer yours first. It's odd when you just ask a person what their name or birthday is without offering yours first.

One common social norm that I have, and am still currently experiencing, is the unsaid, but widely acknowledged [in America] idea that all teenagers need to have a phone. I am not singling out any people when I say this, and I'm definitely not saying that you have to have a phone to have a social life. What I am saying is for kids who don't have phones, especially teenagers, having and maintaining a social life is exponentially harder compared to the kids that do have phones.

I used to have a couple of friends who did not have phones, and they were around my age. During school, I had noticed that their personalities were split into two categories; the kids who didn't interact much in school and the kids who were always interacting in school. I had a theory about this. My theory was: the reason that these kids were split into these two different kinds of groups was because due to their lack of communication (phone), they had not been able to interact with their peers as much as is considered 'normal'. Revolutionary, I know (note the sarcasm).

The kids who fell under the 'didn't interact in school' category, Category A to make things a little easier to follow, most likely were like that because they never got the chance to branch out and experience communication in a way that isn't person to person. I still have many shy friends, and what I've noticed from most of them, is that, if they're shy in person, they are more outgoing through technology, and from what I've seen, it's helped them be more outgoing in person, since the technology allows them to meet new people in a comfortable situation instead of placing them in the very-awkward, face-to-face standard introduction. All the Category A people I've met act very differently than your initial first impression once you get to know them.

So then, why are phones the problem, why can't they branch out on their own? My answer is (most) Category A people are not confident. This makes sense, I met more Category A people when I was in middle school. As a grade-schooler, it was already hard enough to fit in without having to worry about how to stay in touch during the weekends or get phone numbers, but for those students who didn't have phones, well it's easy to see why they became less outgoing in school. Another important note would be that most if not all of the Category A people I've met were introverts. The picture just seems to be getting clearer and clearer.

As for the kids who fell under the 'interact a lot in school' category, we'll call this one Category B, they most likely acted like that because they didn't have the chance to interact with their friends any other way. This may seem like I'm contradicting myself, but I promise my reasoning holds ground. Most if not all of the Category B people I've met were extroverts or ambiverts. This is the biggest difference between the effect of not having a phone between the two types. These kids, as I met most of these people in middle school, were naturally interactive. However, they were also the kids who never got invited to last-minute mall trips or even afterschool trips to the park.

Why?

Because they didn't have a phone number we could easily reach them at (and texting their parents can be intimidating). It wasn't like they could call their parents to ask for permission quickly. So naturally, although Category B kids interacted a lot in school, nobody really got to know them, at least without putting in a tremendous amount of effort. Which, let's be honest, doesn't seem very appealing to a group of middle schoolers just trying to fit in.

I know what you're thinking, 'Why don't their friends try to keep in touch with them in a different way? Email and letters still exist'. That is an extremely reasonable question, unfortunately, kids are extremely unreasonable little people, that includes teenagers.

Finding a teenager willing to go to those lengths to communicate with a peer, especially one they've only known for a year or less, is pretty difficult. That doesn't make teenagers lazy, though. We're just so used to thinking that everyone has a phone, that when we encountered a situation that didn't fit into our box, we avoided it. That mindset is a product of social norms.

Aha! See what I did there?

Just the 'harmless' idea that all teenagers/preteens had phones was enough for some students to change their behavior, as I had just discussed. Imagine some of the bigger social norms that would have a more obvious impact. One example of which would be discussing politics or religion in a casual conversation. Imagine the surprise your conversational partner would be in if you did that.

Though on the other hand, social norms can also do great things. It's not socially normal to be yelling at someone in the middle of a store, and it's not socially normal to go streaking across a Walmart parking lot, so people don't usually do that. The fact that they can be arrested for public indecency most likely helps as well.

The fact of the matter is social norms can do both harm and good. The trick is finding the balance, which I don't think we have yet. Most social norms, contrary to popular belief, are not one size fits all, and what may work for one person or even one group of people will not work for the majority. That's just how it is. However, if we look at them closely enough, social norms are also a fundamental part of society. Despite their diversity, they are so impactful and so important that they also shape the views and personalities of each generation.

Continuing my spiel, another social norm we have is that we always dress according to our environment. I have never attended an awards ceremony in pajamas and I've never gone to the mall with friends in a formal dress. If I think back on it, who was going to stop me if I decided to show up to an award ceremony in a chicken suit? There was no dress code. I could've walked in as a green bean if I wanted to. But I didn't! That is the impact of social norms. Ask yourself, what are you wearing to your next meeting or presentation with your boss? I can already tell you, most likely you're going to show up in formal wear or something equivalent to that.

If those kinds of ideas can affect adults who make a living and survive, it's almost mind-boggling to think about how they affect kids. I've already touched base on this idea, but let's go a little more in-depth with my most controversial idea in this chapter: the social norm to think that kids who do well in school (specifically high school) are more likely to go to college and succeed.

I don't mean to offend anybody who did well or is currently doing well in high school because this is just my personal belief and what I have observed in my short time here on Earth.

I am that kid! I get good grades in school, do extracurriculars, and the teachers like me (hopefully, I wouldn't ask though). I've just noticed that the students who do well in school are told more by their teachers and peers that they're going to be successful when they grow up, compared to the students who are barely getting by. Think about it! Can you think of one instance, where the 'smart' kid was not told by their teacher that they could get into a good school while the struggling student was told they could get in? Let me tell you, I can't.

This puts pressure on the 'smart' kids and makes the struggling students feel like they can't catch up. It's a lose-lose situation. Though of course, it makes sense to think that the kid with the better grades is going to get into the Ivy League school compared to the kid with average grades. However, by separating these kids, the struggling kids are discouraged from even trying. It's important to remember that not every flower blossoms at the same time. And the social norm to just accept that mindset is equally if not more harmful.

Once I laid this entire idea out it was pretty clear to make the decision that 'yeah, that's wrong', but unfortunately, life is rarely ever that simple. What I'm saying is the lack of encouragement towards struggling students may not be as blunt as I illustrated it. In fact, it could even be a little more encouragement for the successful students instead of a lack of encouragement for the struggling students. When I say little, I mean little--just enough to not be obvious, to all parties. It could be a little more slack on subpar assignments or just being called on more in class. Most teachers would hate to learn that they treated their students unfairly, but in reality, that's often the case. It's because of an unconscious mindset shaped by social norms.

I'm not going to pin the blame all on social norms though. A lot of the 'smart' kids work extremely hard, and it's completely understandable that teachers and peers are able to recognize that, we just can't forget about the other students.

As we take a closer look at social norms, we see the impact it has on us as a society. It's crazy to think about, so most people don't. What we may not realize though, is that ideas are always changing and with it, people's mindsets which are formed by social norms. Whether we like it or not, the next generation is not going to think and act like the prior ones, and that's what we have to live with.

I'm truly glad that I had a chance to write this book and talk about life from the perspective of a teenager. I am going to end this chapter with a piece of advice: people are everchanging, so instead of trying to shove everyone in a box, go along with the ride. Thank you for reading.

About the Author

Lauren To is just like any other typical American teenager. She is an author and an avid book-lover. She is also the co-founder of Tutoring by Two, a community-based free math program, and a youth advocate for Evolvement. Through all of her activities, she has gained an immense love for her community and she hopes to make her home a little better of a place step-by-step.

www.ingramcontent.com/pod-product-compliance
Lightning Source LLC
Chambersburg PA
CBHW060255030426
42335CB00014B/1711